XLR8

A PROPHETIC & PRACTICAL *BLUEPRINT*
TO DOUBLE YOUR CHURCH

STUDY GUIDE

Copyright © 2023 by Michael R. Murphy

Published by AVAIL

All rights reserved. No portion of this book may be reproduced, stored in a retrieval system, or transmitted in any form or by any means—electronic, mechanical, photocopy, recording, scanning, or other—except for brief quotations in critical reviews or articles, without prior written permission of the author.

Scripture quotations marked KJV are taken from the King James Version of the Bible. Public domain. Scripture quotations marked NIV are taken from the Holy Bible, New International Version®, NIV®. Copyright © 1973, 1978, 1984, 2011 by Biblica, Inc.™ Used by permission of Zondervan. All rights reserved worldwide. www.zondervan.com. The "NIV" and "New International Version" are trademarks registered in the United States Patent and Trademark Office by Biblica, Inc.™ | Scripture quotations marked NKJV are taken from the New King James Version®. Copyright © 1982 by Thomas Nelson. Used by permission. All rights reserved.

For foreign and subsidiary rights, contact the author.

Cover design by Sara Young
Author photo by Andrew James

ISBN: 978-1-960678-29-4   1 2 3 4 5 6 7 8 9 10

Printed in the United States of America

Author's note: Since this book is being published by an American company, they want to use American spelling and punctuation, at least most of the time. To my Aussie colleagues, I'm not sure if I need to say "Forgive me" or "Get over it." Take your pick.

XLR8

**A PROPHETIC & PRACTICAL *BLUEPRINT*
TO DOUBLE YOUR CHURCH**

MICHAEL R. MURPHY
FOUNDER OF LEADERSCAPE

STUDY GUIDE

CONTENTS

Introduction 7
    Formula 1 10
    Start Your Engines. 14

FIX YOUR NETS 21
    First Gear: Engage Every Guest 22
    Second Gear: Explode Your Growth Track 28

FILL YOUR FUNNEL 35
    Third Gear: Max Your Sunday 36
    Fourth Gear: Mobilize for Mission. 44

FUEL YOUR MULTIPLICATION 49
    Fifth Gear: Empower Your Groups 50
    Sixth Gear: Equip All Leaders. 54

FLEX YOUR CAPACITY 59
    Seventh Gear: Free Your Soul. 60
    Eighth Gear: Fund Your Vision 66

XLR8

A PROPHETIC & PRACTICAL *BLUEPRINT* TO DOUBLE YOUR CHURCH

MICHAEL R. MURPHY
FOUNDER OF LEADERSCAPE

- **FLEX YOUR CAPACITY**
- **FIX YOUR NETS**
- **FUEL YOUR MULTIPLICATION**
- **FILL YOUR FUNNEL**

Gear 8 Fund Your Vision
Gear 1 Engage Every Guest
Gear 7 Free Your Soul
Gear 2 Explode Your Growth Track
Gear 6 Equip All Leaders
Gear 3 Max Your Sunday
Gear 5 Empower Your Groups
Gear 4 Mobilize For Mission

SEAMLESS PROCESS
SPIRITUAL PURPOSE
STRATEGIC PLANS
SUPERNATURAL PRESENCE

XLR8 TRACK
PREVAILING PRAYER

INTRODUCTION

Firstly, congratulations on getting a hold of not just the *XLR8* book, but also the handbook. This indicates a desire to dive deeper and to genuinely immerse yourself in the truths and principles that are going to make a significant difference in the church that you serve. Whether you're a senior pastor, an executive pastor, one of the pastoral team, or one of the key lay leaders, I want to say a big congratulations.

This book is intended to be a companion to the *XLR8* book, not a standalone resource. For that reason, the best way for you and your team to get the most benefit out of this experience, is to read and digest the book, and work parallel handbook.

Next, I want to make some assumptions clear: I assume that you are **consecrated** to the kingdom, that is, that you are someone who has Jesus Christ as the cornerstone for your life and indeed you are called to build His kingdom. Without this underlying philosophy, much of what we write may lack some context and even relevance to you.

Secondly, I'm going to assume that you are called to be a **collaborator** with your pastor to build the local church that he is called to build. Now, though Jesus said, "I will build my church," He never promised to make one disciple. As we obey Him and make disciples, which is what *XLR8* the book and the handbook are about, He will indeed build His church.

As a collaborator, therefore, (the root word of this is co-laborer i.e., someone who comes alongside your pastor and the executive team in order to help), it is very important that we understand that God is a God of order, not of disorder. Should you uncover some things in *XLR8* the book or the handbook, that your church is still on a journey toward implementing, that you handle this in a gracious and uplifting manner and that you realize that not everything needs to or indeed can happen all at once.

One of the things that we are very passionate about at Leaderscape is not only helping leaders know what to do, but know what to do next. You need to be guided by your lead pastor and the executive team of the church as to the timing of what needs to be done when.

The third thing that we're going to assume is that you share a **convergence** with your pastor's vision. That, as a believer, as a leader, as a staff member, you are called to come alongside to support the vision that is the biblical vision to go and make disciples. It is so vital that when you sit in some of the various forums that will unpack this material from the book, you are mindful that you are there to support the vision of the man or the woman that God has set as the leader of the church.

XLR8 the book and the handbook are intended to start, not stop, conversations. Open dialogue and conversations are an important part of learning and indeed embedding the principles that we are confident will help to move your church forward, to get unstuck, and to get moving with fresh moments of making disciples.

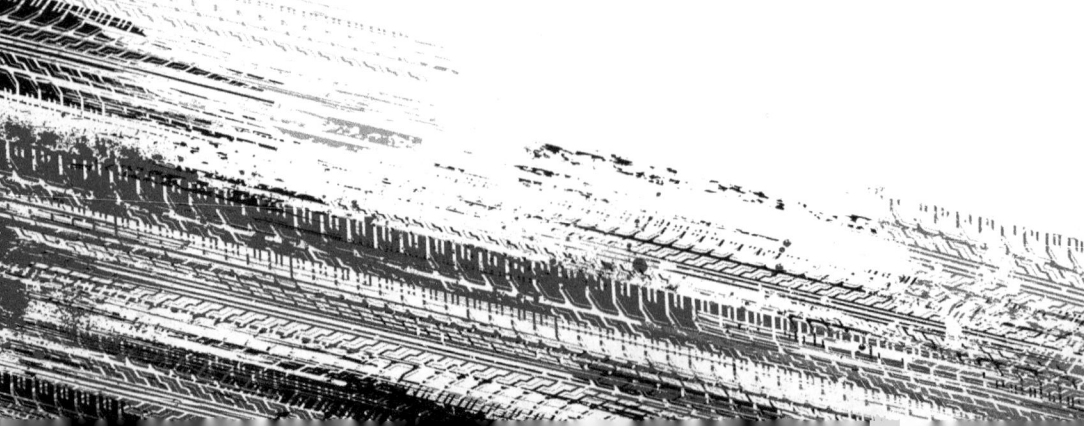

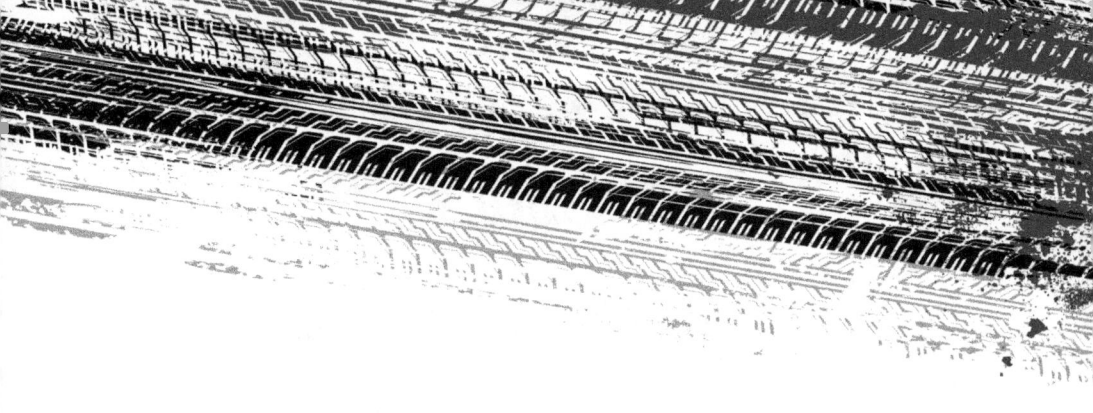

The handbook will quite likely unpack some things as you discuss this together that will require some **course correction**. Many times, these are tweaks to strategies and plans that are already in the pipeline, and indeed, many of the things that you read and discuss will be confirmation of things that God has already been saying. It is true that most many churches have several of the essential components engage individuals and groups in intentional discipleship journeys. What is also true is that many of these components lack coherence and integration. This is where discussing and communicating with the handbook and the book as a foundation can help to make this process seamless.

Culture, it has been said, eats vision for lunch. Having a disciple-making culture in your church is absolutely vital . This handbook can, when used thoroughly, serve to provide a foundation that brings clarity to the kinds of cultural shifts that are necessary for the next season of the church. Your current culture has brought you to where you are right now. It's not unreasonable to imagine that to go to the next level, there will need to be a refinement and some shifts in that culture.

It is our hope and prayer that the pages of this handbook, as you engage with them in a disciplined and comprehensive fashion, will provide a foundation that will help you to actually engage in the action that is necessary to move forward.

FORMULA 1

You're the driver of your F1 car, I'm the mechanic, and your team is the pit crew. The Spirit of God is your fuel.

READING TIME

As you read "Formula 1" in *XLR8*, reflect on, and respond to the text by answering the following questions.

REFLECT AND TAKE ACTION:

Assess the recent momentum of your church and comment on the major impacts of this momentum?

_____
_____
_____
_____
_____
_____
_____
_____
_____

Which two sections of the XLR8 track are you most looking forward to addressing in your Ministry/ Leadership?

_____
_____
_____
_____
_____
_____
_____
_____
_____

> *Therefore, my dear friends, as you have always obeyed—not only in my presence, but now much more in my absence—continue to work out your salvation with fear and trembling, for it is God who works in you to will and to act in order to fulfill his good purpose.*
>
> —Philippians 2:12-13

Consider the scripture above and answer the following questions:

What stands out to you from this passage? What in its meaning applies to your church & leadership momentum right now?

___

What does "His good purpose" mean to you?

___

What does it mean to "work out your salvation with fear and trembling"?

___

Keeping with the F1 motif, if you are the racer, let's identify your pit crew...

- Who are the key members of your pit crew?

_____
_____
_____

- What respective strengths do they bring?

_____
_____
_____
_____

- Are there any skill sets or giftings that are missing or which need to be further developed?

_____
_____
_____
_____

- What area do you feel you and your racing team most need work in and why?

_____
_____
_____
_____

What are the things currently inhibiting your team from going faster?

_____
_____
_____
_____

START YOUR ENGINES

Throughout the Bible, we see leaders plan—and execute their plans—but always led by the Spirit of God.

READING TIME

As you read "Start Your Engines" in *XLR8*, reflect on, and respond to the text by answering the following questions.

REFLECT AND TAKE ACTION:

How do you best prepare for your leadership race as a pastor?

_____
_____
_____
_____
_____
_____
_____

What are the most important elements of preparation?

_____
_____
_____
_____
_____
_____
_____

What is supernatural presence? What are the advantages of this?

_____
_____
_____
_____
_____
_____
_____

Describe any occasions in your own journey when you most experienced God's presence near to you.

___

Do you have a sense of spiritual purpose? Does your church's purpose statement reflect this?

___

What is your vision for the local church God has called you to steward?

___

What are your strategic plans to accomplish? How have these changed since you started?

___

> Be alert and of sober mind. Your enemy the devil prowls around like a roaring lion looking for someone to devour. Resist him, standing firm in the faith, because you know that the family of believers throughout the world is undergoing the same kind of sufferings. And the God of all grace, who called you to his eternal glory in Christ, after you have suffered a little while, will himself restore you and make you strong, firm and steadfast. To him be the power for ever and ever. Amen.
>
> —1 Peter 5:8-11

Consider the scripture above and answer the following questions:

For every plan God gives us, the enemy of our soul attempts to thwart them with an opposing plan. What are some of these schemes which you can recognize that have been arrayed against you over these past few years?

_____
_____
_____
_____
_____
_____

What stands out to you from this verse?

_____
_____
_____
_____
_____

According to this verse, how can we resist our adversary?

_____
_____
_____
_____

How would you define the culture of your organization?

_____
_____
_____
_____

How do you as the leader set the precedent for and maintain culture?

_____
_____
_____
_____
_____

What do your daily habits look like? Are there any negative habits you need to change?

_____
_____
_____
_____
_____
_____
_____

Do you have daily confessions? How might adding these to your routine benefit you?

_____
_____
_____
_____
_____
_____
_____

FIX YOUR NETS

FIRST GEAR: ENGAGE EVERY GUEST

A judicious, excellent, focused, warm welcome to roll out the red carpet for "new friends" of the church—guests or visitors—makes an indelible impression and begins a heart-to-heart engagement leading, hopefully, to genuine discipleship.

READING TIME

As you read "First Gear: Engage Every Guest" in *XLR8*, reflect on, and respond to the text by answering the following questions.

REFLECT AND TAKE ACTION:

How does your church **currently** engage new guests?

_____
_____
_____
_____

How would you currently rate your engagement on a scale of 1-10?

1   2   3   4   5   6   7   8   9   10

Has your engagement always been on this level?

_____
_____
_____
_____

What strategies from this chapter can help your organization increase its engagement?

_____
_____
_____
_____
_____

> *May the God who gives endurance and encouragement give you the same attitude of mind toward each other that Chris Jesus had, so that with one mind and one voice you may glorify the God and Father of our Lord Jesus Christ. Accept one another, then, just as Christ accepted you, in order to bring praise to God.*
>
> **—Romans 15:5-7**

Consider the scripture above and answer the following questions:

How do you think the meaning of this verse relates to your guest engagement that pleases the heart of God?

_____
_____
_____
_____

According to this verse, what are we supposed to do once God gives us "the same attitude of mind toward each other that Christ Jesus had"?

_____
_____
_____
_____

What steps can you take to ensure each engagement opportunity remains an "awkward-free zone"?

_____
_____
_____
_____

Have you or your team ever blown it in one of the ways listed in this chapter? Describe the situation.

_____
_____
_____
_____
_____
_____

Of the four engagement strategies provided, which do you and your pit crew need to work on most?

_____
_____
_____
_____
_____

Take time to do a sensory walkthrough of your church's engagement elements. Is the text on the sign too small? What do they see first in the lobby?

_____
_____
_____
_____
_____

Does your VIP team have a clearly scripted approach to greeting and engaging with new guests? Why or why not?

_____
_____

How well are you drawing the various streams of contact information from new guests (guest cards/ kids church registrations/first-time givers/first-time small group registrations) into a single river?

What is the current percentage of guest cards in relation to attendance? What would be the difference in the annual number of guests between your current percentage and our 4 percent Leaderscape benchmark?

How well is the VIP team developing the early stages of trust with guests?

_____
_____
_____
_____

- How could this positively shift? _____

_____
_____
_____
_____

What's happening at the front door? How well is your VIP team welcoming guests?

_____
_____
_____
_____
_____

SECOND GEAR: EXPLODE YOUR GROWTH TRACK

Vulnerability is the currency of engagement.

READING TIME

As you read "Second Gear: Explode Your Growth Track" in *XLR8*, reflect on, and respond to the text by answering the following questions.

REFLECT AND TAKE ACTION:

Do you **currently** have a culture of disciple-making **as a church**? Do people understand that their purpose is to deepen and expand God's kingdom?

_____
_____
_____
_____
_____
_____
_____

What percentage of your people are in small groups? _____

What is your current number of groups? _____

- What is this as a percentage of your:
    - Weekend attendance: _____
    - Men: _____
    - Women: _____
    - Children: _____

How effectively is your growth track being led?

_____
_____
_____
_____
_____
_____

XLR8: STUDY GUIDE | 29

- In what ways are the leaders welcoming new people?

___

- Is it curated for connection?

___

Are the current leaders of your church's Growth Track leading it in a way that will effectively see 80 percent of those who enter it get planted in Small groups?

___

Take time to read over the three-meeting model. What stands out to you from each week of communication?

- Week #1:_____
  _____

- Week #2:_____
  _____

- Week #3:_____
  _____

How can you apply the above principles to the next three meetings within your own church? Write your plan for each week below.

- Week #1:_____
  _____
  _____
  _____
  _____
  _____

- Week #2:_____
  _____
  _____
  _____
  _____

- Week #3:_____
_____
_____
_____
_____

With your three-week plan in mind, read through the list of mistakes that pastors can make when they launch a Growth Track, and adjust your plan accordingly.

- Week #1:_____
_____
_____
_____

- Week #2:_____
_____
_____
_____

- Week #3:_____
_____
_____
_____

Is your Growth Track warm, inspiring, and informative? Is it led well? What is the ambiance?

_____
_____
_____
_____

Are your people trained to bring people to Growth Track, not just tell them about it?

_____
_____
_____
_____

What results are you hoping for through the execution of your Growth Track?

_____
_____
_____
_____

FILL YOUR FUNNEL

THIRD GEAR: MAX YOUR SUNDAY

It's important to identify your target audience.

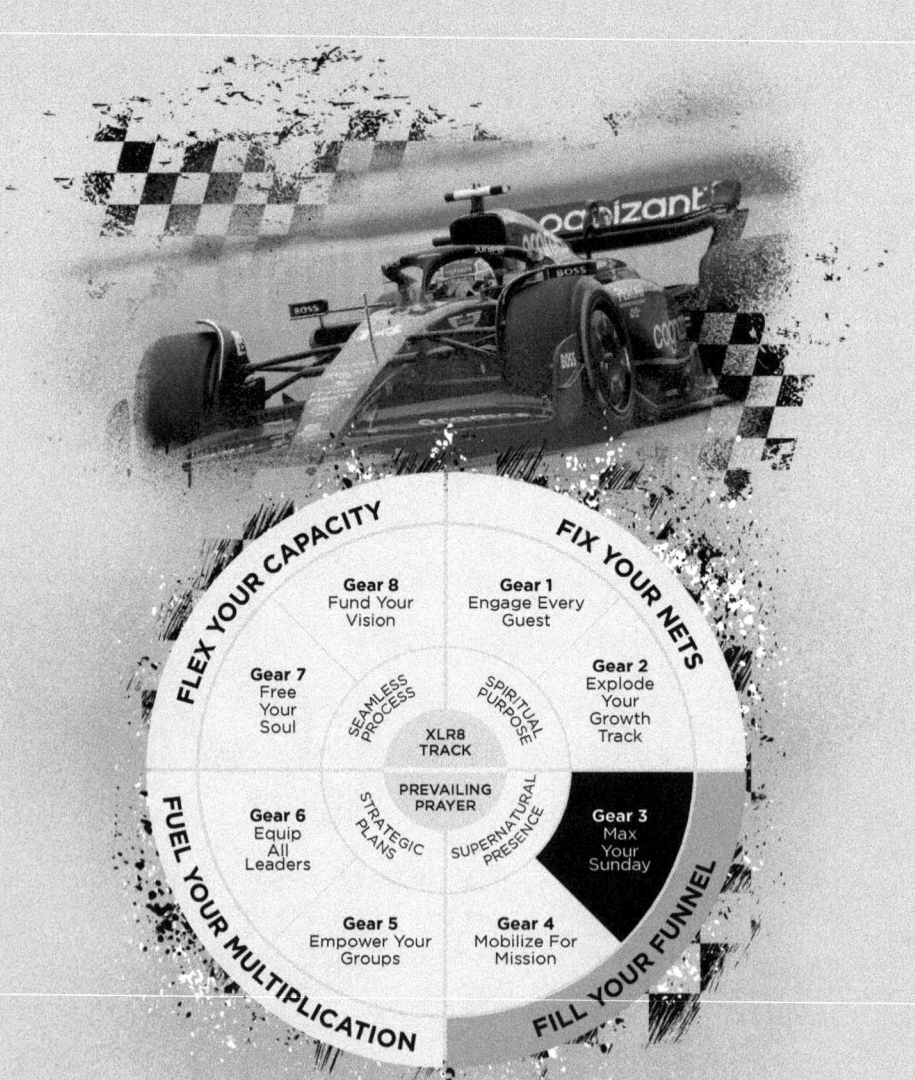

READING TIME

As you read "Third Gear: Max Your Sunday" in *XLR8*, reflect on, and respond to the text by answering the following questions.

REFLECT AND TAKE ACTION:

Who is your target audience on Sundays?

_____
_____
_____
_____

What can you do differently to better "**maximize** your Sunday"?

_____
_____
_____
_____
_____

How effective and thorough is your weekly FORMAL post-Sunday debrief?

_____
_____
_____
_____
_____

What online presence does your church have? Do you stream weekly?

_____
_____
_____
_____
_____

- Is the reach of this currently growing or is it static? _____
- What specific things are you doing to turn your online audience into an engaged part of your church family? _____

_____
_____
_____
_____

Is the physical appearance of the exterior of your church property well maintained? How does the building look from the outside?

_____
_____
_____
_____

Do you have your best people on the greeting and VIP teams? What are people's first impressions when they enter the building?

_____
_____
_____
_____

How is your children's program? Do they have a separate area? How could you improve it?

_____
_____
_____
_____
_____

What is the look and feel of the front door to the children's area?

_____
_____
_____
_____
_____

What is the current state of your auditorium? Does it have enough seating? Lighting?

_____
_____
_____
_____
_____

> *"The Spirit of the Lord is on me, because he has anointed me to proclaim good news to the poor. He has sent me to proclaim freedom for the prisoners and recovery of sight for the blind, to set the oppressed free, to proclaim the year of the Lord's favor."*
>
> —Luke 4:18-19

Consider the scripture above and answer the following questions:

What is the meaning of this verse?

_____
_____
_____
_____
_____

How can this verse be applied to you accelerating your church and in particular "Maxing your Sunday"?

_____
_____
_____
_____
_____

What is your priority when preaching and teaching God's word?

_____
_____
_____
_____
_____

How do you currently assess how effective you are at preaching and teaching the word each week?

_____
_____
_____
_____

- What additional assessments could you add to help you improve as a communicator of the gospel?_____

_____
_____
_____
_____

- What specific things are you engaged in to become a better preacher? _____

_____
_____
_____
_____

How much time do you spend praying the message into your heart once you have completed studying for the delivery?

_____
_____
_____
_____

How do you communicate the gospel of the kingdom?

_____
_____
_____
_____
_____

Do you make your messages relatable to those who have little to no spiritual background?

_____
_____
_____
_____
_____

How can you better create experiences through the service?

_____
_____
_____
_____
_____
_____
_____

"For the word of God is living and powerful, and sharper than any two-edged sword, piercing even to the division of soul and spirit, and of joints and marrow, and is a discerner of the thoughts and intents of the heart. And there is no creature hidden from His sight, but all things are naked and open to the eyes of Him to whom we must give account"

—Hebrews 4:12-13

FOURTH GEAR: MOBILIZE FOR MISSION

It should be no different for believers in every generation.

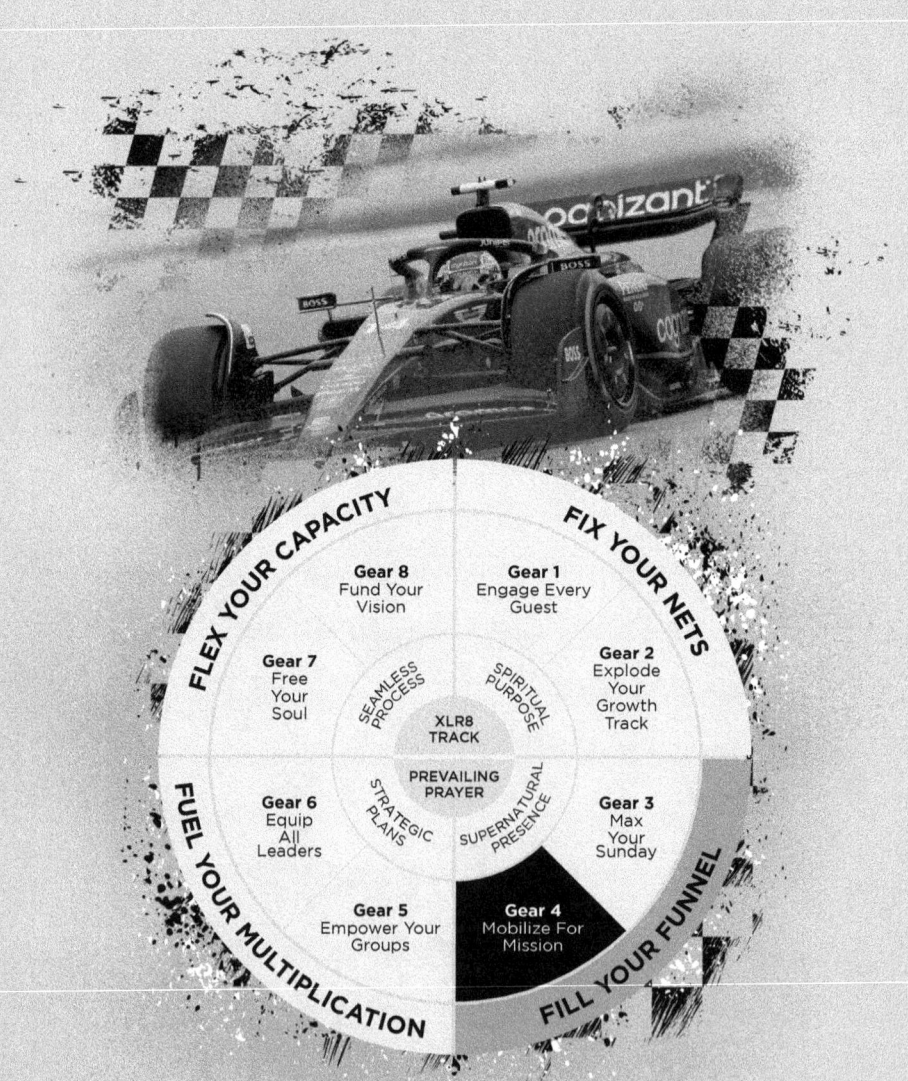

READING TIME

As you read "Fourth Gear: Mobilize for Mission" in *XLR8*, reflect on, and respond to the text by answering the following questions.

REFLECT AND TAKE ACTION:

What is church momentum and why is it important?

_____
_____
_____
_____

> But you are a chosen people, a royal priesthood, a holy nation, God's special possession, that you may declare the praises of him who called you out of darkness into his wonderful light. Once you were not a people, but now you are the people of God; once you had not received mercy, but now you have received mercy.
>
> —1 Peter 2:9-10

Consider the scripture above and answer the following questions:

What stands out to you about this verse?

_____
_____
_____
_____

How does this verse motivate or inspire you?

_____
_____
_____
_____

10 DIAGNOSTIC QUESTIONS TO ASSESS YOUR MOMENTUM

Answer 1-10: 1 being very poor and 10 being absolutely brilliant (Circle one)

1) How would you rate the level of fullness of your soul right now?

   1   2   3   4   5   6   7   8   9   10

2) How strongly are the mission and vision of your church informing the schedule and activity of you and your team?

   1   2   3   4   5   6   7   8   9   10

3) How effectively is a significant percentage of your church actively mobilized and engaged in reaching new people?

   1   2   3   4   5   6   7   8   9   10

4) How full is the onramp "funnel" of your church with new visitors, guests, and viewers right now?

   1   2   3   4   5   6   7   8   9   10

5) How effective is your current Growth Track at converting at least thirty percent of new identified guests into your small group attendees and/or dream team members?

   1   2   3   4   5   6   7   8   9   10

6) How well is your church connecting and engaging with new visitors and viewers in both the online and in-person spaces?

       1   2   3   4   5   6   7   8   9   10

7) How strongly are your current number and health of your small groups and dream teams positioned to take the church forward right now?

       1   2   3   4   5   6   7   8   9   10

8) How clear and effective is the current development plan for your own leadership?

       1   2   3   4   5   6   7   8   9   10

9) How effective is your current Leadership Development Pipeline at intentionally raising three deep leaders across the church?

       1   2   3   4   5   6   7   8   9   10

10) How would you rate the current overall momentum trajectory of your church?

       1   2   3   4   5   6   7   8   9   10

From these assessments, which area do you need to work on most?

Look at the list of solutions provided at the end of this chapter. What is a practical way your church can solve the problem and spark momentum?

FUEL YOUR MULTIPLICATION

FIFTH GEAR: EMPOWER YOUR GROUPS

Church services generally aren't designed to create and build community.

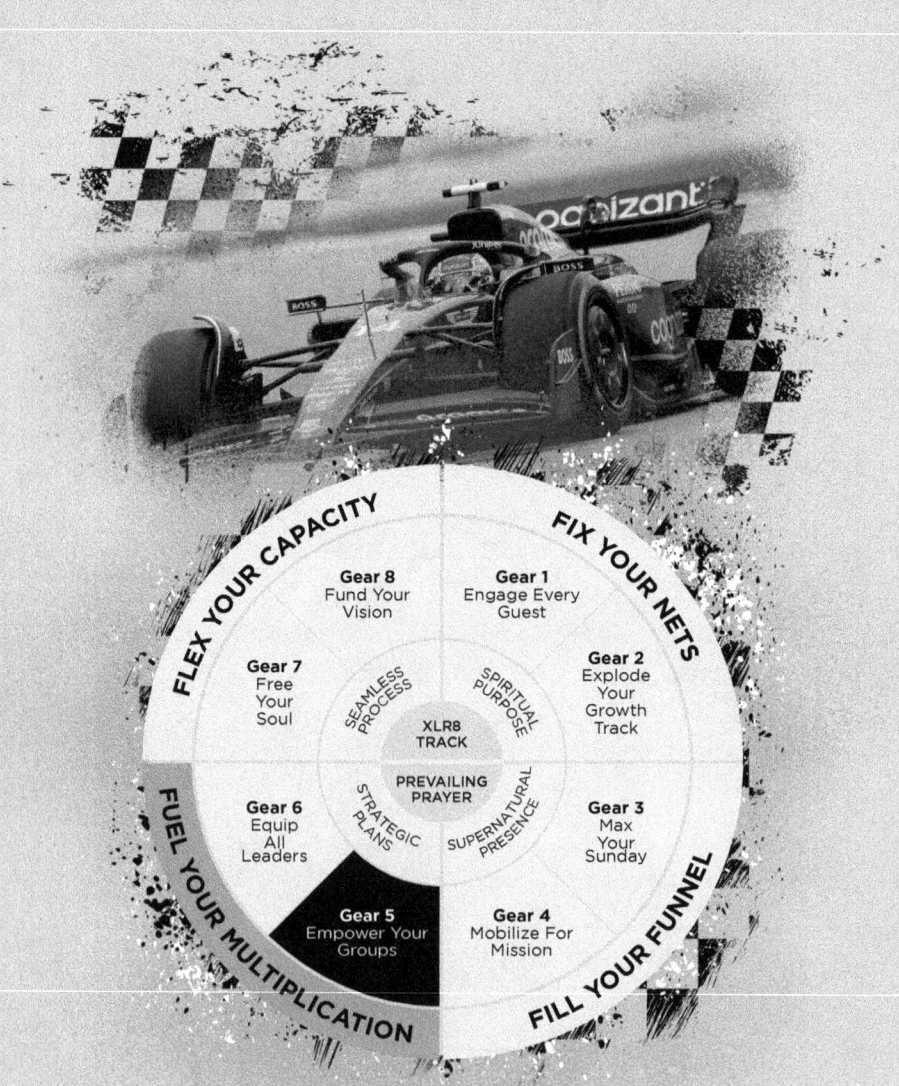

READING TIME

As you read "Fifth Gear: Empower Your Groups" in *XLR8*, reflect on, and respond to the text by answering the following questions.

REFLECT AND TAKE ACTION:

Are there leaders in your church who really grasp the concept of multiplication? Who?

_____
_____
_____
_____

What do the above leaders have that others don't?

_____
_____
_____
_____

- How well do they understand how to do the following:
    - Grow their group_____
    _____
    - Build a life-giving atmosphere_____
    _____
    - Handle challenging people_____
    _____
    - Triage a crisis_____
    _____
    - Move each person one step_____
    _____

- How many of the groups are actually looking to multiply next semester?_____
_____

Do you consider your church to be a life-giving environment? Why or why not?

_____
_____
_____
_____

How intentional are your Group leaders in helping everyone take the next step in their spiritual journey? How can you do this better moving forward?

_____
_____
_____
_____

Are there any leaders or individuals you feel you should equip to lead a group? Who and why?

_____
_____
_____
_____

What do you personally do to get on mission every week?

_____
_____
_____
_____

How will you implement the four purposes described in this chapter?

1) Create a life-giving environment:_____
_____
_____

2) Move everyone one step:_____
_____
_____

3) Build leadership three deep:_____
_____
_____

4) Get on mission every week:_____
_____
_____

- What do you expect should happen?_____
_____
_____

SIXTH GEAR: EQUIP ALL LEADERS

When we train group leaders, we're equipping them to have a profound impact on individuals, families, communities, and the world.

READING TIME

As you read "Sixth Gear: Equip All Leaders" in *XLR8*, reflect on, and respond to the text by answering the following questions.

REFLECT AND TAKE ACTION:

Why is creating a group atmosphere important? How is a group atmosphere created?

_____
_____
_____
_____
_____
_____
_____

How can a leader catalyze group-centric growth? What does it mean to be group-centric?

_____
_____
_____
_____
_____
_____
_____

How can a leader connect people? Why is this valuable?

_____
_____
_____
_____
_____
_____
_____

What does it mean to "curate spiritual potency"? How does one do this?

_____
_____
_____
_____
_____
_____

How can a leader encourage group engagement? Is this the only way?

_____
_____
_____
_____
_____

What does it mean to manage group dynamics?

_____
_____
_____
_____
_____

How can a leader effectively handle someone who is being difficult?

_____
_____
_____
_____
_____
_____
_____

What is a "triaging life crisis"? What is an effective way to respond to this?

_____
_____
_____
_____
_____
_____
_____

How can a leader help everyone take their next discipleship steps? What happens if a leader does not do this?

_____
_____
_____

How can a leader effectively help others uncover their callings?

What can a leader to do mobilize members?

What do you think is the single biggest key to raising up new leaders?

FLEX YOUR CAPACITY

SEVENTH GEAR: FREE YOUR SOUL

The truth of the gospel, applied to our deepest wounds and highest hopes, sets us free, but we need to know how to apply it.

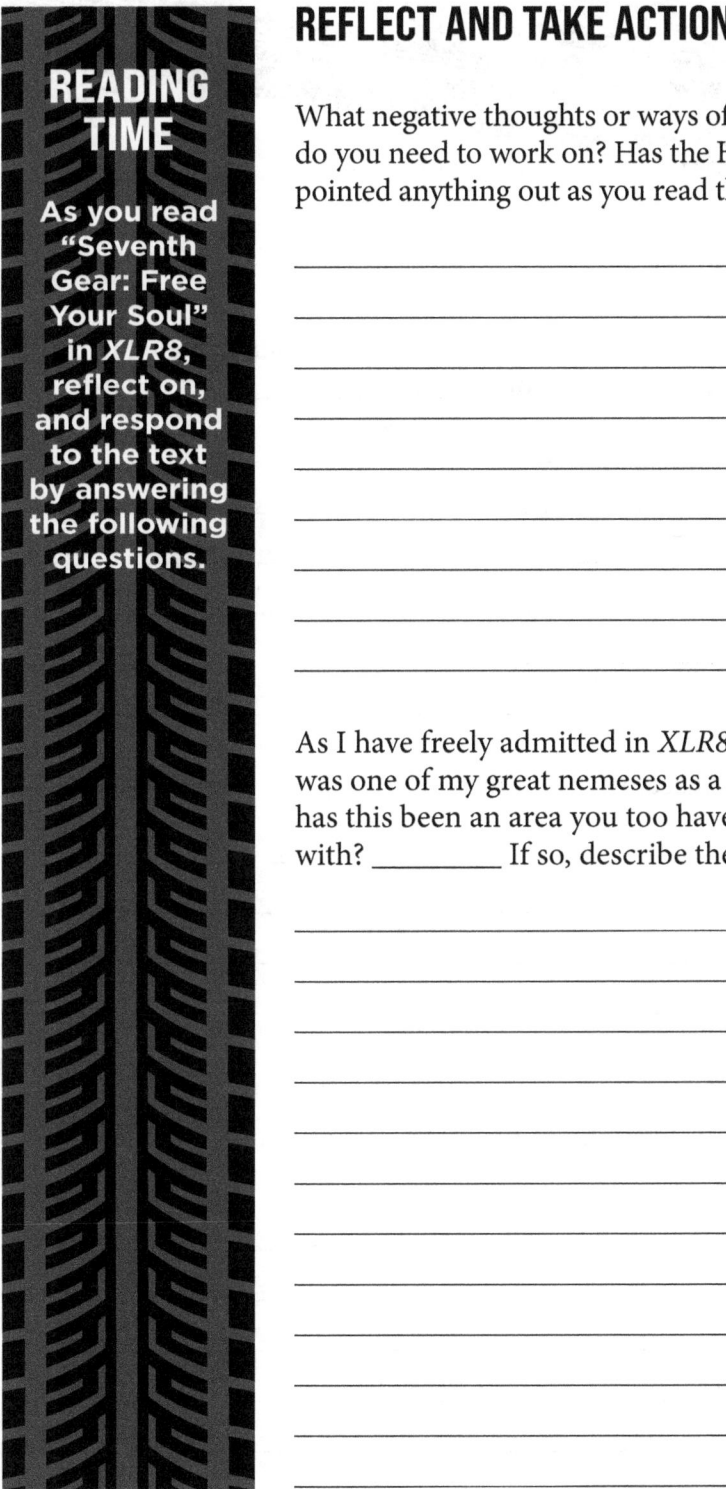

READING TIME

As you read "Seventh Gear: Free Your Soul" in *XLR8*, reflect on, and respond to the text by answering the following questions.

REFLECT AND TAKE ACTION:

What negative thoughts or ways of thinking do you need to work on? Has the Holy Spirit pointed anything out as you read this chapter?

_____
_____
_____
_____
_____
_____
_____
_____

As I have freely admitted in *XLR8*, insecurity was one of my great nemeses as a leader. . . . has this been an area you too have struggled with? _____ If so, describe the situation.

_____
_____
_____
_____
_____
_____
_____
_____
_____
_____

Do you see any of the signs of an insecure leader provided in this chapter in you or other leaders?_____ Explain.

_____
_____
_____
_____
_____
_____

Where does insecurity stem from?

_____
_____
_____
_____
_____

How can you invest more productively in your soul? When will you start?

_____
_____
_____
_____
_____

> This is what the LORD says: "Let not the wise boast of their wisdom or the strong boast of their strength or the rich boast of their riches, but let the one who boasts boast about this: that they have the understanding to know me, that I am the LORD, who exercises kindness, justice and righteousness on earth, for in these I delight," declares the LORD.
>
> —Jeremiah 9:23-24

Consider the scripture above and answer the following questions:

What does this verse reveal about boasting?

_____
_____
_____
_____
_____
_____
_____
_____

What is the meaning of this passage?

_____
_____
_____
_____
_____
_____
_____
_____

What does Paul mean when he wrote "war according to the flesh" to the Corinthians?

_____
_____
_____
_____
_____
_____

What other passages from this chapter stood out to you?

_____
_____
_____
_____
_____
_____
_____
_____
_____
_____
_____
_____

What strongholds have you toppled with God's help in the past?

_____
_____
_____
_____
_____
_____
_____
_____
_____
_____

Have you been owning your morning since the Formula 1 chapter? _____ If you have, what difference has this made? If you haven't, what difference do you think it will make?

_____
_____
_____
_____
_____
_____

EIGHTH GEAR: FUND YOUR VISION

We need to understand the distinction between the Giver and the givers.

READING TIME

As you read "Eighth Gear: Fund Your Vision" in *XLR8*, reflect on, and respond to the text by answering the following questions.

REFLECT AND TAKE ACTION:

What is the difference between the Giver and the givers?

_____
_____
_____
_____
_____

> The LORD had said to Abram, "Go from your country, your people and your father's household to the land I will show you. "I will make you into a great nation, and I will bless you; I will make your name great, And you will be a blessing. I will bless those who bless you, and whoever curses you I will curse; and all peoples on earth will be blessed through you."
> —Genesis 12:1-3

Consider the scripture above and answer the following questions:

How is God's generosity revealed through this passage?

_____
_____
_____
_____
_____
_____

Take time to fill out the "Financial Strength Diagnostic" provided at *Pit Stop* at the end of the chapter

What are your lowest scoring categories in the diagnostic? Which were your highest?

_____
_____
_____
_____
_____
_____
_____
_____
_____
_____
_____

Fill out the "comprehensive road map" at the end of the chapter

Fill out the exercise under "Worksheet on Generosity"

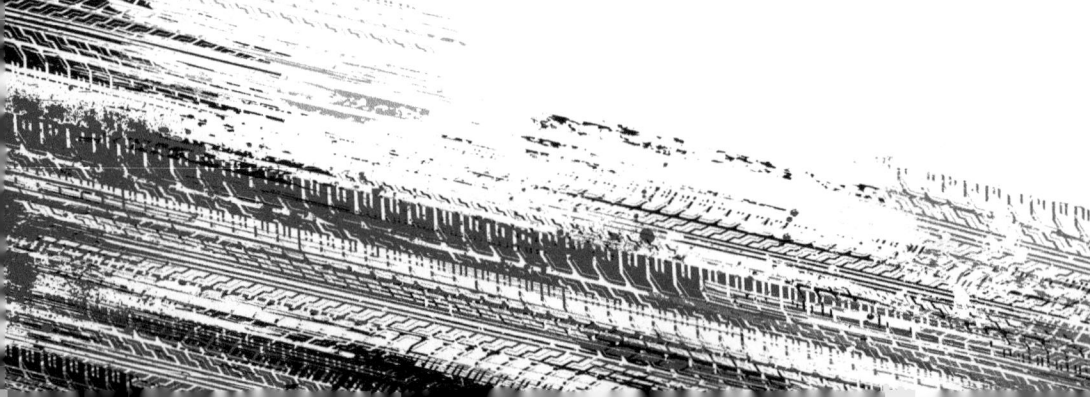

What is your church's average weekly attendance? _____

How many "giving units" do you have? _____

What is the average household income for your community?
_____

What does this exercise tell you?
_____
_____
_____
_____
_____
_____

What is your plan to increase the level of cheerful giving at your church?
_____
_____
_____
_____
_____
_____

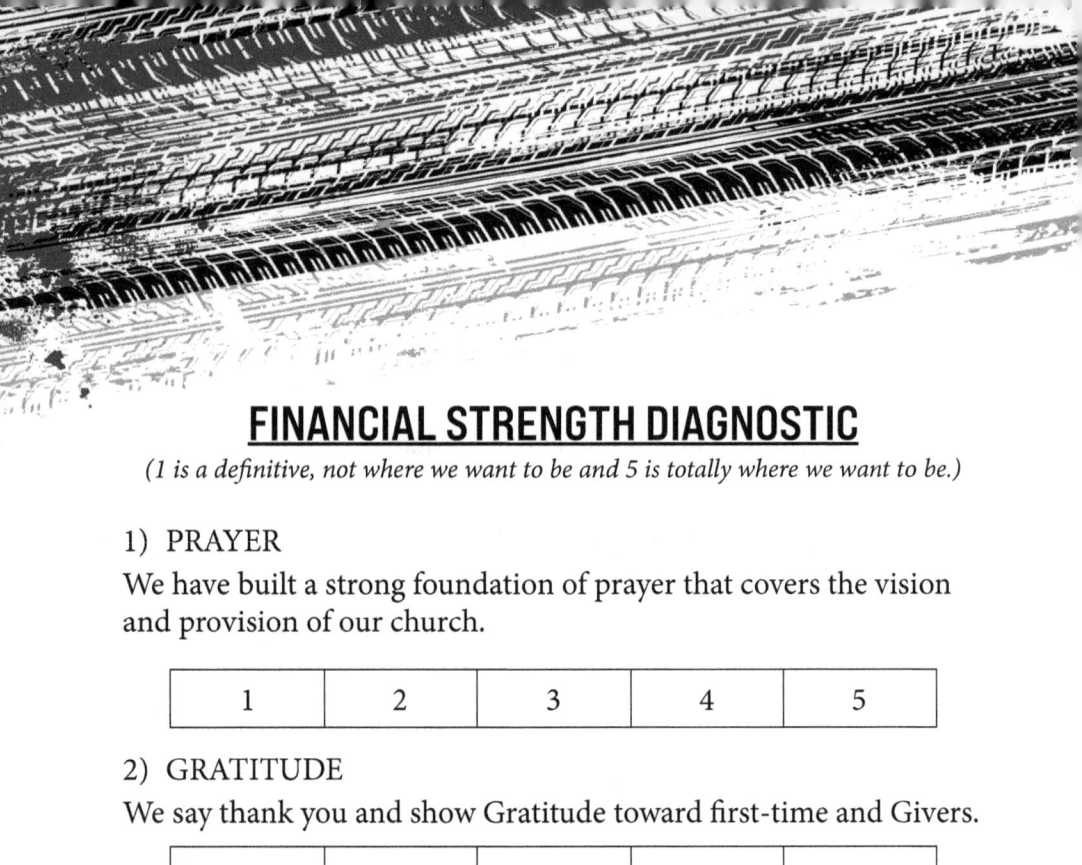

FINANCIAL STRENGTH DIAGNOSTIC

(1 is a definitive, not where we want to be and 5 is totally where we want to be.)

1) PRAYER
We have built a strong foundation of prayer that covers the vision and provision of our church.

1	2	3	4	5

2) GRATITUDE
We say thank you and show Gratitude toward first-time and Givers.

1	2	3	4	5

3) ENCOUNTER
We relentlessly pursue powerful encounters and transformation for all people.

1	2	3	4	5

4) UNITY
We have a strong sense and reality of relational and missional unity from the elders, pastors, and leaders through to the congregation members.

1	2	3	4	5

5) TRUTH
We courageously impart the truth of God's Word about finance and stewardship.

1	2	3	4	5

6) SERIES

We preach a series on giving and generosity each year, which we also carry through and integrate through our Small Groups.

1	2	3	4	5

7) ENGAGEMENT

We are building a strong community of marketplace leaders.

1	2	3	4	5

8) GENERATIONS

We have a vibrant ministry to children and teens to which they regularly bring their friends.

1	2	3	4	5

9) MINISTRY

We are leading a ministry that sees people transformed by the power and Word of God.

1	2	3	4	5

10) GROUPS

We have a well-developed and effective small group ministry that has built genuine connectedness amongst the hearts and lives of the people.

1	2	3	4	5

11) DISCIPLESHIP
We make and hold a clear connection between stewardship and discipleship.

1	2	3	4	5

12) CELEBRATION
We conduct weekend services at our church that are Christ-centered, Bible-based, and accommodating of both guests and those already committed to the church.

1	2	3	4	5

13) COMMUNITY
We meet real and desperate needs in both our local community and in the nations.

1	2	3	4	5

14) INTENTIONALITY
We minister to and partner intentionally with business and marketplace leaders in our church.

1	2	3	4	5

15) VISION
We carry a vision that captivates and resonates with the people in our church.

1	2	3	4	5

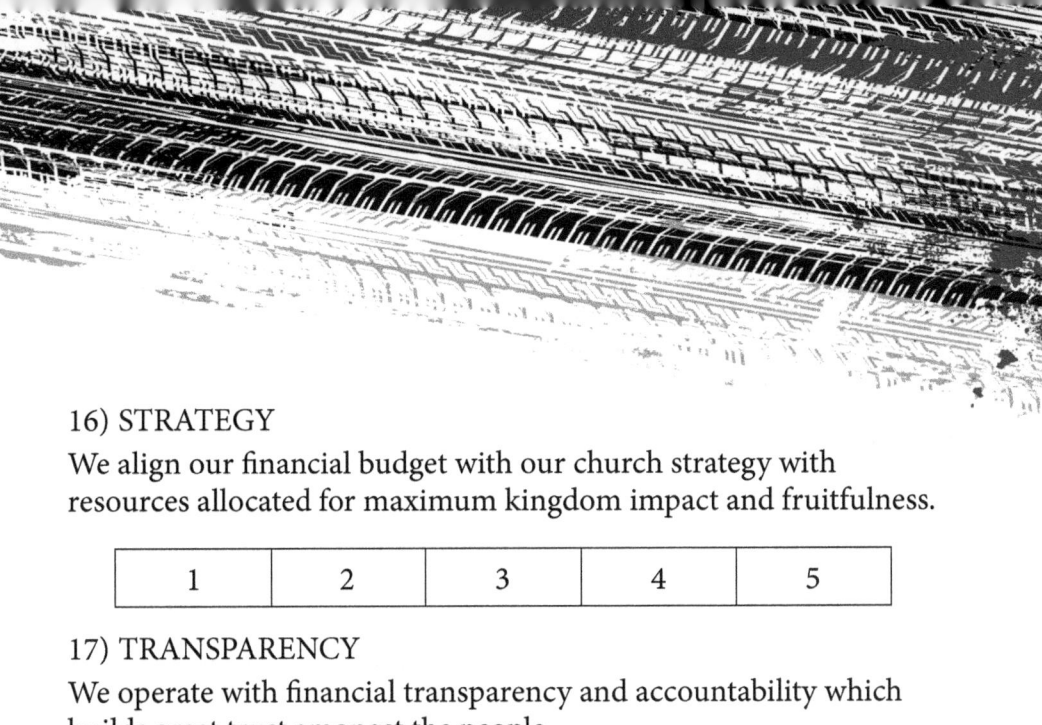

16) STRATEGY

We align our financial budget with our church strategy with resources allocated for maximum kingdom impact and fruitfulness.

1	2	3	4	5

17) TRANSPARENCY

We operate with financial transparency and accountability which builds great trust amongst the people.

1	2	3	4	5

18) FRUITFULNESS

We have a demonstrated track record of strong ministry fruitfulness.

1	2	3	4	5

19) THE LEAST

We minister effectively to the "least," the poor, and the vulnerable in our community.

1	2	3	4	5

20) KINGDOM BUILDERS

We have developed a strong kingdom builders ministry who understand that part of their reason for existing is to resource the kingdom of God.

1	2	3	4	5

www.ingramcontent.com/pod-product-compliance
Lightning Source LLC
Chambersburg PA
CBHW062121080426
42734CB00012B/2947